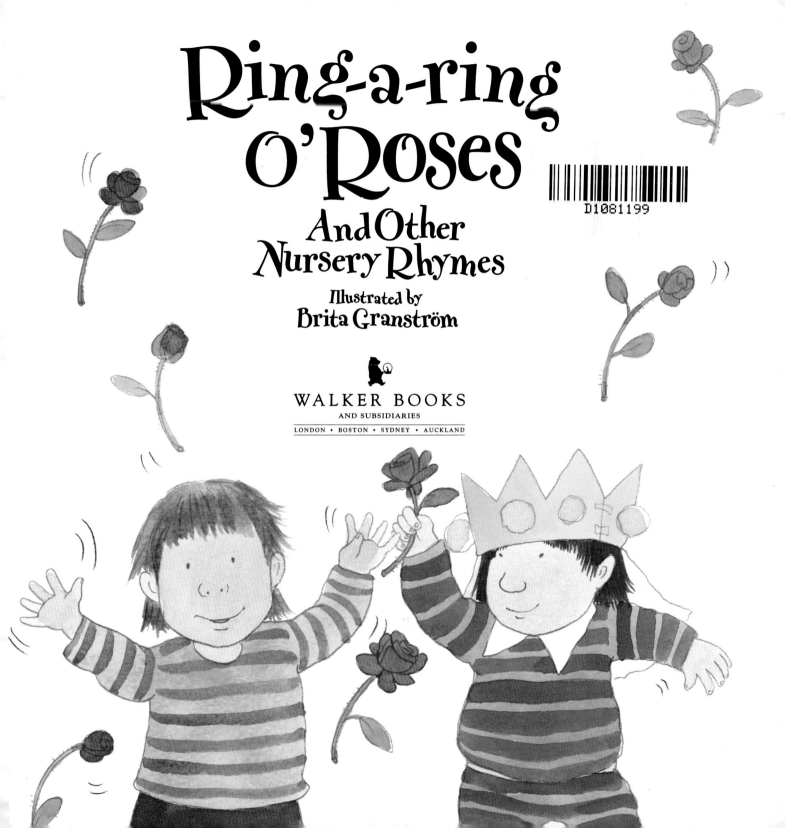

Ring-a-ring O'Roses
And Other Nursery Rhymes

Illustrated by
Brita Granström

WALKER BOOKS
AND SUBSIDIARIES
LONDON • BOSTON • SYDNEY • AUCKLAND

D1081199

Little Miss Muffet
Sat on a tuffet,
Eating her curds
and whey;
There came a
big spider,
Who sat down
beside her …

Old King Cole
Was a merry old soul,
And a merry old soul
was he;
He called for his pipe,
And he called for
his bowl …

three.

Lavender's blue,
dilly, dilly,
Lavender's green;
When I am king,
dilly, dilly ...

queen.

Pussy cat, pussy cat,
Where have you been?
I've been to London
To look at the Queen.
Pussy cat, pussy cat,
What did you there? ...

I frightened
a little mouse
Under her chair.

Ring-a-ring o' roses,
A pocket full of posies,
A-tishoo! A-tishoo! ...

down!

Georgie Porgie
pudding and pie,
Kissed the girls
and made them cry;
When the boys
came out to play ...

ran away.

Little Boy Blue,
Come blow your horn,
The sheep's in the
meadow,
The cow's in the corn;
But where is the boy
Who looks after the
sheep? …

haystack,

Teddy bear, teddy bear, turn around.
Teddy bear, teddy bear, touch the ground.
Teddy bear, teddy bear, turn out the light.
Teddy bear, teddy bear, say …

Goodnight!

For Cameron,
Chloe, James and Max!
With love
B.G.

First published 1999 by Walker Books Ltd
87 Vauxhall Walk, London SE11 5HJ

This edition published 2008

2 4 6 8 10 9 7 5 3 1

This collection © Walker Books

Illustrations © 1999 Brita Granström

The moral rights of the illustrator have been asserted.

This book has been typeset in Times.

Printed in China

British Library Cataloguing in Publication Data:
a catalogue record for this book is available from the British Library.

ISBN 978-1-4063-1683-4

www.walkerbooks.co.uk